POETRY FROM CRESCENT MOON

William Shakespeare: *Selected Sonnets and Verse*
edited, with an introduction by Mark Tuley

William Shakespeare: *The Sonnets*
edited and introduced by Mark Tuley

*Shakespeare: Love, Poetry and Magic
in Shakespeare's Sonnets and Plays*
by B.D. Barnacle

Edmund Spenser: *Heavenly Love: Selected Poems*
selected and introduced by Teresa Page

Robert Herrick: *Delight In Disorder: Selected Poems*
edited and introduced by M.K. Pace

Sir Thomas Wyatt: *Love For Love: Selected Poems*
selected and introduced by Louise Cooper

John Donne: *Air and Angels: Selected Poems*
selected and introduced by A.H. Ninham

D.H. Lawrence: *Being Alive: Selected Poems*
edited with an introduction by Margaret Elvy

D.H. Lawrence: Symbolic Landscapes
by Jane Foster

D.H. Lawrence: Infinite Sensual Violence
by M.K. Pace

Percy Bysshe Shelley: *Paradise of Golden Lights: Selected Poems*
selected and introduced by Charlotte Greene

Thomas Hardy: *Her Haunting Ground: Selected Poems*
edited, with an introduction by A.H. Ninham

Sexing Hardy: Thomas Hardy and Feminism
by Margaret Elvy

Emily Bronte: *Darkness and Glory: Selected Poems*
selected and introduced by Miriam Chalk

John Keats: *Bright Star: Selected Poems*
edited with an introduction by Miriam Chalk

Henry Vaughan: *A Great Ring of Pure and Endless Light: Selected Poems*
selected and introduced by A.H. Ninham

The Crescent Moon Book of Love Poetry
edited by Louise Cooper

The Crescent Moon Book of Mystical Poetry in English
edited by Carol Appleby

The Crescent Moon Book of Nature Poetry From Langland to Lawrence
edited by Margaret Elvy

The Crescent Moon Book of Metaphysical Poetry
edited and introduced by Charlotte Greene

The Crescent Moon Book of Elizabethan Love Poetry
edited and introduced by Carol Appleby

The Crescent Moon Book of Romantic Poetry
edited and introduced by L.M. Poole

Blinded By Her Light The Love-Poetry of Robert Graves
by Jeremy Mark Robinson

The Best of Peter Redgrove's Poetry: The Book of Wonders
by Peter Redgrove, edited and introduced by Jeremy Mark Robinson

Peter Redgrove: Here Comes the Flood
by Jeremy Mark Robinson

Sex-Magic-Poetry-Cornwall: A Flood of Poems
by Peter Redgrove, edited with an essay by Jeremy Mark Robinson

Brigitte's Blue Heart
by Jeremy Reed

Claudia Schiffer's Red Shoes
by Jeremy Reed

By-Blows: Uncollected Poems
by D.J. Enright

Petrarch, Dante and the Troubadours: The Religion of Love and Poetry
by Cassidy Hughes

Dante: *Selections From the Vita Nuova*
translated by Thomas Okey

Arthur Rimbaud: *Selected Poems*
edited and translated by Andrew Jary

Arthur Rimbaud: *A Season in Hell*
edited and translated by Andrew Jary

Rimbaud: Arthur Rimbaud and the Magic of Poetry
by Jeremy Mark Robinson

Friedrich Hölderlin: *Hölderlin's Songs of Light: Selected Poems*
translated by Michael Hamburger

Rainer Maria Rilke: *Dance the Orange:* Selected Poems
translated by Michael Hamburger

Rilke: Space, Essence and Angels in the Poetry of Rainer Maria Rilke
by B.D. Barnacle

German Romantic Poetry: Goethe, Novalis,
Heine, Hölderlin, Schlegel, Schiller
by Carol Appleby

Arseny Tarkovsky: *Life, Life: Selected Poems*
translated by Virginia Rounding

Emily Dickinson: *Wild Nights: Selected Poems*
selected and introduced by Miriam Chalk

Cavafy: Anatomy of a Soul
by Matt Crispin

THE VISIONS OF
PETRARCH AND BELLAY
EARLY SONNETS

THE VISIONS OF PETRARCH AND BELLAY EARLY SONNETS

Edmund Spenser

Edited by Teresa Page

CRESCENT MOON

CRESCENT MOON PUBLISHING
P.O. Box 1312, Maidstone
Kent, ME14 5XU
Grerat Britain

First published 2018.

Printed and bound in the U.S.A.
Set in Book 11 on 14pt.
Designed by Radiance Graphics.

The right of Teresa Page to be identified as the editor of this book has been asserted generally in accordance with sections 77 and 78 of the Copyright, Designs and Patents Act 1988.

All rights reserved. No part of this book may be reprinted or reproduced, stored in a retrieval system, or transmitted, in any form or by any means, electronic, mechanical, photocopying, recording or otherwise, without permission from the publisher.

British Library Cataloguing in Publication data
Spenser, Edmund
The Visions of Petrarch and Bellay. - (British Poets Series)
I. Title II. Page, Teresa
III. Series
821.3

ISBN-13 9781861717214

CONTENTS

The Visions of Petrarch ✻ 15
The Visions of Bellay ✻ 25
The Ruins of Rome ✻ 43
A Note On Edmund Spenser ✻ 85
Notes ✻ 91
Further Reading ✻ 94

NOTE ON THE TEXT

The text is from *The Poetical Works of Edmund Spenser*, volume 5, and the sections: *The Ruins of Rome, The Visions of Bellay* and *The Vision of Petrarch*.

Edmund Spenser

Elizabeth I, anonymous artist, 1575,
National Portrait Gallery, London

THE VISIONS OF PETRARCH[1]

---
[1] Translated from Clement Marot's French edition of Francesco Petrarch's *Rime Sparse*.

I

Being one day at my window all alone,
So manie strange things happened me to see,
As much it grieveth me to thinke thereon.
At my right hand a hynde appear'd to mee.
So faire as mote the greatest god delite;
Two eager dogs did her pursue in chace,
Of which the one was blacke, the other white.
With deadly force so in their cruell race
They pincht the haunches of that gentle beast,
That at the last, and in short time, I spide,
Under a rocke, where she, alas! opprest,
Fell to the ground, and there untimely dide.
  Cruell death vanquishing so noble beautie,
  Oft makes me wayle so hard a destenie.

II

After, at sea a tall ship did appeare,
Made all of heben and white yvorie;
The sailes of golde, of silke the tackle were.
Milde was the winde, calme seem'd the sea to bee,
The skie eachwhere did show full bright and faire:
With rich treasures this gay ship fraighted was:
But sudden storme did so turmoyle the aire,
And tumbled up the sea, that she, alas!
Strake on a rock, that under water lay,
And perished past all recoverie.
O! how great ruth, and sorrow-full assay,
Doth vex my spirite with perplexitie,
  Thus in a moment to see lost and drown'd
  So great riches as like cannot be found.

III

The heavenly branches did I see arise
Out of the fresh and lustie lawrell tree,
Amidst the yong greene wood: of Paradise
Some noble plant I thought my selfe to see.
Such store of birds therein yshrowded were,
Chaunting in shade their sundrie melodie,
That with their sweetnes I was ravish't nere.
While on this lawrell fixed was mine eie,
The skie gan everie where to overcast,
And darkned was the welkin all about,
When sudden flash of heavens fire out brast,
And rent this royall tree quite by the roote;
  Which makes me much and ever to complaine,
  For no such shadow shalbe had againe.

IV

Within this wood, out of a rocke did rise
A spring of water, mildly rumbling downe,
Whereto approched not in anie wise
The homely shepheard, nor the ruder clowne;
But manie Muses, and the Nymphes withall,
That sweetly in accord did tune their voyce
To the soft sounding of the waters fall;
That my glad hart thereat did much reioyce.
But, while herein I tooke my chiefe delight,
I saw, alas! the gaping earth devoure
The spring, the place, and all cleane out of sight;
Which yet aggreeves my hart even to this houre,
  And wounds my soule with rufull memorie,
  To see such pleasures gon so suddenly.

V

I saw a Phoenix in the wood alone,
With purple wings and crest of golden hewe;
Strange bird he was, whereby I thought anone
That of some heavenly wight I had the vewe;
Untill he came unto the broken tree,
And to the spring that late devoured was.
What say I more? Each thing at last we see
Doth passe away: the Phoenix there, alas!
Spying the tree destroid, the water dride,
Himselfe smote with his beake, as in disdaine,
And so foorthwith in great despight he dide;
That yet my heart burnes in exceeding paine
  For ruth and pitie of so haples plight.
  O, let mine eyes no more see such a sight!

VI

At last, so faire a ladie did I spie,
That thinking yet on her I burne and quake:
On hearbs and flowres she walked pensively;
Milde, but yet love she proudly did forsake:
White seem'd her robes, yet woven so they were
As snow and golde together had been wrought:
Above the wast a darke clowde shrouded her.
A stinging serpent by the heele her caught;
Wherewith she languisht as the gathered floure,
And, well assur'd, she mounted up to ioy.
Alas! on earth so nothing doth endure,
But bitter griefe and sorrowfull annoy:
  Which make this life wretched and miserable.
  Tossed with stormes of fortune variable.

VII

When I behold this tickle trustles state
Of vaine worlds glorie, flitting too and fro,
And mortall men tossed by troublous fate
In restles seas of wretchednes and woe,
I wish I might this wearie life forgoe,
And shortly turne unto my happie rest,
Where my free spirite might not anie moe
Be vest with sights that doo her peace molest.
And ye, faire Ladie, in whose bounteous brest
All heavenly grace and vertue shrined is,
When ye these rythmes doo read, and vew the rest,
Loath this base world, and thinke of heavens blis:
  And though ye be the fairest of Gods creatures,
  Yet thinke that death shall spoyle your goodly features.

THE VISIONS OF BELLAY

I

It was the time when rest, soft sliding downe
From heavens hight into mens heavy eyes,
In the forgetfulnes of sleepe doth drowne
The carefull thoughts of mortall miseries.
Then did a ghost before mine eyes appeare,
On that great rivers banck that runnes by Rome;
Which, calling me by name, bad me to reare
My lookes to heaven whence all good gifts do come,
And crying lowd, "Loe! now beholde," quoth hee,
"What under this great temple placed is:
Lo, all is nought but flying vanitee!"
So I, that know this worlds inconstancies,
  Sith onely God surmounts all times decay,
  In God alone my confidence do stay.

II

On high hills top I saw a stately frame,
An hundred cubits high by iust assize,
With hundreth pillours fronting faire the same,
All wrought with diamond after Dorick wize.
Nor brick nor marble was the wall in view,
But shining christall, which from top to base
Out of her womb a thousand rayons threw
On hundred steps of Afrike golds enchase.
Golde was the parget, and the seeling bright
Did shine all scaly with great plates of golde;
The floore of iasp and emeraude was dight.
O worlds vainesse! Whiles thus I did behold,
  An earthquake shooke the hill from lowest seat,
  And overthrew this frame with ruine great.

III

Then did a sharped spyre of diamond bright,
Ten feete each way in square, appeare to mee,
Iustly proportion'd up unto his hight,
So far as archer might his level see.
The top thereof a pot did seeme to beare,
Made of the mettall which we most do honour;
And in this golden vessel couched weare
The ashes of a mightie emperour:
Upon foure corners of the base were pight,
To beare the frame, foure great lyons of gold;
A worthy tombe for such a worthy wight.
Alas! this world doth nought but grievance hold:
  I saw a tempest from the heaven descend,
  Which this brave monument with flash did rend.

IV

I saw raysde up on yvorie pillowes tall,
Whose bases were of richest mettalls warke,
The chapters alablaster, the fryses christall,
The double front of a triumphall arke.
On each side purtraid was a Victorie,
Clad like a nimph, that wings of silver weares,
And in triumphant chayre was set on hie,
The auncient glory of the Romaine peares.
No worke it seem'd of earthly craftsmans wit,
But rather wrought by his owne industry
That thunder-dartes for Iove his syre doth fit.
Let me no more see faire thing under sky,
  Sith that mine eyes have seene so faire a sight
  With sodain fall to dust consumed quight.

V

Then was the faire Dodonian tree far seene
Upon seaven hills to spread his gladsome gleame,
And conquerours bedecked with his greene,
Along the bancks of the Ausonian streame.
There many an aunciente trophee was addrest,
And many a spoyle, and many a goodly show,
Which that brave races greatnes did attest,
That whilome from the Troyan blood did flow.
Ravisht I was so rare a thing to vew;
When lo! a barbarous troupe of clownish fone
The honour of these noble boughs down threw:
Under the wedge I heard the tronck to grone;
  And since, I saw the roote in great disdaine
  A twinne of forked trees send forth againe.

VI

I saw a wolfe under a rockie cave
Noursing two whelpes; I saw her litle ones
In wanton dalliance the teate to crave,
While she her neck wreath'd from them for the nones.
I saw her raunge abroad to seeke her food,
And roming through the field with greedie rage
T'embrew her teeth and clawes with lukewarm blood
Of the small heards, her thirst for to asswage.
I saw a thousand huntsmen, which descended
Downe from the mountaines bordring Lombardie,
That with an hundred speares her flank wide rened:
I saw her on the plaine outstretched lie,
  Throwing out thousand throbs in her owne soyle:
  Soone on a tree uphang'd I saw her spoyle.

VII

I saw the bird that can the sun endure
With feeble wings assay to mount on hight;
By more and more she gan her wings t'assure,
Following th'ensample of her mothers sight.
I saw her rise, and with a larger flight
To pierce the cloudes, and with wide pinneons
To measure the most haughtie mountaines hight,
Untill she raught the gods owne mansions.
There was she lost; when suddaine I behelde,
Where, tumbling through the ayre in firie fold,
All flaming downe she on the plaine was felde,
And soone her bodie turn'd to ashes colde.
  I saw the foule that doth the light dispise
  Out of her dust like to a worme arise.

VIII

I saw a river swift, whose fomy billowes
Did wash the ground-work of an old great wall;
I saw it cover'd all with griesly shadowes,
That with black horror did the ayre appall:
Thereout a strange beast with seven heads arose,
That townes and castles under her brest did coure,
And seem'd both milder beasts and fiercer foes
Alike with equall ravine to devoure.
Much was I mazde to see this monsters kinde
In hundred formes to change his fearefull hew;
When as at length I saw the wrathfull winde,
Which blows cold storms, burst out of Scithian mew,
  That sperst these cloudes; and, in so short as thought,
  This dreadfull shape was vanished to nought.

IX

Then all astonied with this mighty ghoast,
An hideous bodie, big and strong, I sawe,
With side long beard, and locks down hanging loast,
Sterne face, and front full of Satúrnlike awe;
Who, leaning on the belly of a pot,
Pourd foorth a water, whose out gushing flood
Ran bathing all the creakie shore aflot,
Whereon the Troyan prince spilt Turnus blood;
And at his feete a bitch wolfe suck did yeeld
To two young babes: his left the palme tree stout,
His right hand did the peacefull olive wield.
And head with lawrell garnisht was about.
 Sudden both palme and olive fell away,
 And faire green lawrell branch did quite decay.

X

Hard by a rivers side a virgin faire,
Folding her armes to heaven with thousand throbs,
And outraging her cheekes and golden haire,
To falling rivers sound thus tun'd her sobs.
"Where is," quoth she, "this whilom honoured face?
Where the great glorie and the auncient praise,
In which all worlds felicitie had place,
When gods and men my honour up did raise?
Suffisd' it not that civill warres me made
The whole worlds spoile, but that this Hydra new,
Of hundred Hercules to be assaide,
With seven heads, budding monstrous crimes anew,
  So many Neroes and Caligulaes
  Out of these crooked shores must dayly rayse?"

XI

Upon an hill a bright flame I did see,
Waving aloft with triple point to skie,
Which, like incense of precious cedar tree,
With balmie odours fil'd th'ayre farre and nie.
A bird all white, well feathered on each wing,
Hereout up to the throne of gods did flie,
And all the way most pleasant notes did sing,
Whilst in the smoake she unto heaven did stie.
Of this faire fire the scattered rayes forth threw
On everie side a thousand shining beames:
When sudden dropping of a silver dew
(O grievous chance!) gan quench those precious flames;
  That it, which earst so pleasant sent did yeld,
  Of nothing now but noyous sulphure smeld.

XII

I saw a spring out of a rocke forth rayle,
As cleare as christall gainst the sunnie beames;
The bottome yeallow, like the golden grayle
That bright Pactolus washeth with his streames.
It seem'd that Art and Nature had assembled
All pleasure there for which mans hart could long;
And there a noyse alluring sleepe soft trembled,
Of manie accords, more sweete than mermaids song,
The seates and benches shone as yvorie,
And hundred nymphes sate side by side about;
When from nigh hills, with hideous outcrie,
A troupe of satyres in the place did rout,
Which with their villeine feete the streame did ray,
Threw down the seats, and drove the nymphs away.

XIII

Much richer then that vessell seem'd to bee
Which did to that sad Florentine appeare,
Casting mine eyes farre off, I chaunst to see
Upon the Latine coast herselfe to reare.
But suddenly arose a tempest great,
Bearing close envie to these riches rare,
Which gan assaile this ship with dreadfull threat,
This ship, to which none other might compare:
And finally the storme impetuous
Sunke up these riches, second unto none,
Within the gulfe of greedie Nereus.
I saw both ship and mariners each one,
  And all that treasure, drowned in the maine:
  But I the ship saw after raisd' againe.

XIV

Long having deeply gron'd these visions sad,
I saw a citie like unto that same
Which saw the messenger of tidings glad,
But that on sand was built the goodly frame:
It seem'd her top the firmament did rayse,
And, no lesse rich than faire, right worthie sure
(If ought here worthie) of immortall dayes,
Or if ought under heaven might firme endure.
Much wondred I to see so faire a wall:
When from the Northerns coast a storme arose,
Which, breathing furie from his inward gall
On all which did against his course oppose,
  Into a clowde of dust sperst in the aire
  The weake foundations of this citie faire.

XV

At length, even at the time when Morpheus
Most trulie doth unto our eyes appeare,
Wearie to see the heavens still wavering thus,
I saw Typhaeus sister comming neare;
Whose head, full bravely with a morion hidd,
Did seeme to match the gods in maiestie.
She, by a rivers bancke that swift downe slidd,
Over all the world did raise a trophee hie;
An hundred vanquisht kings under her lay,
With armes bound at their backs in shamefull wize.
Whilst I thus mazed was with great affray,
I saw the heavens in warre against her rize:
  Then downe she stricken fell with clap of thonder,
  That with great noyse I wakte in sudden wonder.

RUINS OF ROME[2]

BY JOACHIM DU BELLAY

---
[2] Translated from Joachim du Bellay's *Le Premier Livre des Antiquez de Rome.*

I

Ye heavenly spirites, whose ashie cinders lie
Under deep ruines, with huge walls opprest,
But not your praise, the which shall never die
Through your faire verses, ne in ashes rest;
If so be shrilling voyce of wight alive
May reach from hence to depth of darkest hell,
Then let those deep abysses open rive,
That ye may understand my shreiking yell!
Thrice having seene under the heavens veale
Your toombs devoted compasse over all,
Thrice unto you with lowd voyce I appeale,
And for your antique furie here doo call,
  The whiles that I with sacred horror sing
  Your glorie, fairest of all earthly thing!

II

Great Babylon her haughtie walls will praise,
And sharped steeples high shot up in ayre;
Greece will the olde Ephesian buildings blaze,
And Nylus nurslings their Pyramides faire;
The same yet vaunting Greece will tell the storie
Of Ioves great image in Olympus placed;
Mausolus worke will be the Carians glorie,
And Crete will boast the Labyrinth, now raced;
The antique Rhodian will likewise set forth
The great Colosse, erect to Memorie;
And what els in the world is of like worth,
Some greater learned wit will magnifie.
  But I will sing above all moniments
  Seven Romane Hils, the worlds seven wonderments.

III

Thou stranger, which for Rome in Rome hero seekest,
And nought of Rome in Rome perceiv'st at all,
These same olde walls, olde arches, which thou seest,
Olde palaces, is that which Rome men call.
Beholde what wreake, what mine, and what wast,
And how that she which with her mightie powre
Tam'd all the world hath tam'd herselfe at last;
The pray of Time, which all things doth devowre!
Rome now of Rome is th'onely funerall,
And onely Rome of Rome hath victorie;
Ne ought save Tyber hastning to his fall
Remaines of all: O worlds inconstancie!
  That which is firme doth flit and fall away,
  And that is flitting doth abide and stay.

IV

She whose high top above the starres did sore,
One foote on Thetis, th'other on the Morning,
One hand on Scythia, th'other on the More,
Both heaven and earth in roundnesse compassing;
Iove fearing, least if she should greater growe,
The old giants should once againe uprise,
Her whelm'd with hills, these seven hils, which be nowe
Tombes of her greatnes which did threate the skies:
Upon her head he heapt Mount Saturnal,
Upon her bellie th'antique Palatine,
Upon her stomacke laid Mount Quirinal,
On her left hand the noysome Esquiline,
  And Caelian on the right; but both her feete
  Mount Viminal and Aventine doo meete.

V

Who lists to see what ever nature, arte,
And heaven could doo, O Rome, thee let him see,
In case thy greatnes he can gesse in harte
By that which but the picture is of thee!
Rome is no more: but if the shade of Rome
May of the bodie yeeld a seeming sight,
It's like a corse drawne forth out of the tombe
By magicke skill out of eternall night:
The corpes of Rome in ashes is entombed,
And her great spirite, reioyned to the spirite
Of this great masse, is in the same enwombed;
But her brave writings, which, her famous merite
  In spight of Time out of the dust doth reare,
  Doo make her idole through the world appeare.

VI

Such as the Berecynthian goddesse bright,
In her swifte charret with high turrets crownde,
Proud that so manie gods she brought to light,
Such was this citie in her good daies fownd:
This citie, more than that great Phrygian mother
Renowm'd for fruite of famous progenie,
Whose greatnes by the greatnes of none other,
But by her selfe, her equall match could see:
Rome onely might to Rome compared bee,
And onely Rome could make great Rome to tremble:
So did the gods by heavenly doome decree,
That other earthlie power should not resemble
  Her that did match the whole earths puissaunce,
  And did her courage to the heavens advaunce.

VII

Ye sacred ruines, and ye tragick sights,
Which onely doo the name of Rome retaine,
Olde moniments, which of so famous sprights
The honour yet in ashes doo maintaine,
Triumphant arcks, spyres neighbours to the skie,
That you to see doth th'heaven it selfe appall,
Alas! by little ye to nothing flie,
The peoples fable, and the spoyle of all!
And though your frames do for a time make warre
Gainst Time, yet Time in time shall ruinate
Your workes and names, and your last reliques marre.
My sad desires, rest therefore moderate!
  For if that Time make ende of things so sure,
  It als will end the paine which I endure.

VIII

Through armes and vassals Rome the world subdu'd,
That one would weene that one sole cities strength
Both land and sea in roundnes had survew'd,
To be the measure of her bredth and length:
This peoples vertue yet so fruitfull was
Of vertuous nephewes, that posteritie,
Striving in power their grandfathers to passe,
The lowest earth ioin'd to the heaven hie;
To th'end that, having all parts in their power,
Nought from the Romane Empire might be quight;
And that though Time doth commonwealths devowre,
Yet no time should so low embase their hight,
  That her head, earth'd in her foundations deep,
  Should not her name and endles honour keep.

IX

Ye cruell starres, and eke ye gods unkinde,
Heaven envious, and bitter stepdame Nature!
Be it by fortune, or by course of kinde,
That ye doo weld th'affaires of earthlie creature;
Why have your hands long sithence traveiled
To frame this world, that doth endure so long?
Or why were not these Romane palaces
Made of some matter no lesse firme and strong?
I say not, as the common voyce doth say,
That all things which beneath the moone have being
Are temporall and subiect to decay:
But I say rather, though not all agreeing
  With some that weene the contrarie in thought,
  That all this whole shall one day come to nought.

X

As that brave sonne of Aeson, which by charmes
Atcheiv'd the golden fleece in Colchid land,
Out of the earth engendred men of armes
Of dragons teeth, sowne in the sacred sand,
So this brave towne, that in her youthlie daies
An hydra was of warriours glorious,
Did fill with her renowmed nourslings praise
The firie sunnes both one and other hous:
But they at last, there being then not living
An Hercules so ranke seed to represse,
Emongst themselves with cruell furie striving,
Mow'd downe themselves with slaughter mercilesse;
  Renewing in themselves that rage unkinde,
  Which whilom did those earthborn brethren blinde.

XI

Mars, shaming to have given so great head
To his off-spring, that mortall puissaunce,
Puft up with pride of Romane hardiehead,
Seem'd above heavens powre it selfe to advaunce,
Cooling againe his former kindled heate
With which he had those Romane spirits fild.
Did blowe new fire, and with enflamed breath
Into the Gothicke colde hot rage instil'd.
Then gan that nation, th'earths new giant brood,
To dart abroad the thunderbolts of warre,
And, beating downe these walls with furious mood
Into her mothers bosome, all did marre;
  To th'end that none, all were it Iove his sire,
  Should boast himselfe of the Romane empire.

XII

Like as whilome the children of the earth
Heapt hils on hils to scale the starrie skie,
And fight against the gods of heavenly berth,
Whiles Iove at them his thunderbolts let flie;
All suddenly with lightning overthrowne,
The furious squadrons downe to ground did fall,
That th'earth under her childrens weight did grone,
And th'heavens in glorie triumpht over all;
So did that haughtie front, which heaped was
On these seven Romane hils, it selfe upreare
Over the world, and lift her loftie face
Against the heaven, that gan her force to feare.
  But now these scorned fields bemone her fall,
  And gods secure feare not her force at all.

XIII

Nor the swift furie of the flames aspiring,
Nor the deep wounds of victours raging blade,
Nor ruthlesse spoyle of souldiers blood-desiring,
The which so oft thee, Rome, their conquest made,
Ne stroke on stroke of fortune variable,
Ne rust of age hating continuance,
Nor wrath of gods, nor spight of men unstable,
Nor thou oppos'd against thine owne puissance,
Nor th'horrible uprore of windes high blowing,
Nor swelling streames of that god snakie-paced
Which hath so often with his overflowing
Thee drenched, have thy pride so much abaced,
  But that this nothing, which they have thee left,
  Makes the world wonder what they from thee reft.

XIV

As men in summer fearles passe the foord
Which is in winter lord of all the plaine,
And with his tumbling streames doth beare aboord
The ploughmans hope and shepheards labour vaine,
And as the coward beasts use to despise
The noble lion after his lives end,
Whetting their teeth, and with vaine foolhardise
Daring the foe that cannot him defend,
And as at Troy most dastards of the Greekes
Did brave about the corpes of Hector colde,
So those which whilome wont with pallid cheekes
The Romane triumphs glorie to behold,
  Now on these ashie tombes shew boldnesse vaine,
  And, conquer'd, dare the conquerour disdaine.

XV

Ye pallid spirits, and ye ashie ghoasts,
Which, ioying in the brightnes of your day,
Brought foorth those signes of your presumptuous boasts
Which now their dusty reliques do bewray,
Tell me, ye spirits! (sith the darksome river
Of Styx, not passable to soules returning,
Enclosing you in thrice three wards for ever,
Doo not restraine your images still mourning,)
Tell me then, (for perhaps some one of you
Yet here above him secretly doth hide,)
Doo ye not feele your torments to accrewe,
When ye sometimes behold the ruin'd pride
  Of these old Romane works, built with your hands,
  To become nought els but heaped sands?

XVI

Like as ye see the wrathfull sea from farre
In a great mountaine heap't with hideous noyse,
Eftsoones of thousand billowes shouldred narre,
Against a rocke to breake with dreadfull poyse;
Like as ye see fell Boreas with sharpe blast
Tossing huge tempests through the troubled skie,
Eftsoones having his wide wings spent in wast,
To stop his wearie cariere suddenly;
And as ye see huge flames spred diverslie,
Gathered in one up to the heavens to spyre,
Eftsoones consum'd to fall downe feebily,
So whilom did this monarchie aspyre
  As waves, as winde, as fire, spred over all,
  Till it by fatall doome adowne did fall.

XVII

So long as Ioves great bird did make his flight,
Bearing the fire with which heaven doth us fray,
Heaven had not feare of that presumptuous might,
With which the giaunts did the gods assay:
But all so soone as scortching sunne had brent
His wings which wont the earth to overspredd,
The earth out of her massie wombe forth sent
That antique horror which made heaven adredd.
Then was the Germane raven in disguise
That Romane eagle seene to cleave asunder,
And towards heaven freshly to arise
Out of these mountaines, now consum'd to pouder.
  In which the foule that serves to beare the lightning
  Is now no more seen flying nor alighting.

XVIII

These heapes of stones, these old wals which ye see,
Were first enclosures but of salvage soyle;
And these brave pallaces, which maystred bee
Of time, were shepheards cottages somewhile.
Then tooke the shepheards kingly ornaments
And the stout hynde arm'd his right hand with steele:
Eftsoones their rule of yearely presidents
Grew great, and six months greater a great deele;
Which, made perpetuall, rose to so great might,
That thence th'imperiall eagle rooting tooke,
Till th'heaven it selfe, opposing gainst her might,
Her power to Peters successor betooke,
  Who, shepheardlike, (as Fates the same foreseeing,)
  Doth shew that all things turne to their first being.

XIX

All that is perfect, which th'heaven beautefies;
All that's imperfect, borne belowe the moone;
All that doth feede our spirits and our eies;
And all that doth consume our pleasures soone;
All the mishap the which our daies outweares;
All the good hap of th'oldest times afore,
Rome, in the time of her great ancesters,
Like a Pandora, locked long in store.
But destinie this huge chaos turmoyling,
In which all good and evill was enclosed,
Their heavenly vertues from these woes assoyling,
Caried to heaven, from sinfull bondage losed:
  But their great sinnes, the causers of their paine,
  Under these antique ruines yet remaine.

XX

No otherwise than raynie cloud, first fed
With earthly vapours gathered in the ayre,
Eftsoones in compas arch't, to steepe his hed,
Doth plonge himselfe in Tethys bosome faire,
And, mounting up againe from whence he came,
With his great bellie spreds the dimmed world,
Till at the last, dissolving his moist frame,
In raine, or snowe, or haile, he forth is horld,
This citie, which was first but shepheards shade,
Uprising by degrees, grewe to such height
That queene of land and sea her selfe she made.
At last, not able to beare so great weight,
  Her power, disperst, through all the world did vade;
  To shew that all in th'end to nought shall fade.

XXI

The same which Pyrrhus and the puissaunce
Of Afrike could not tame, that same brave citie
Which, with stout courage arm'd against mischaunce,
Sustein'd the shocke of common enmitie,
Long as her ship, tost with so manie freakes,
Had all the world in armes against her bent,
Was never seene that anie fortunes wreakes
Could breake her course begun with brave intent.
But, when the obiect of her vertue failed,
Her power it selfe against it selfe did arme;
As he that having long in tempest sailed
Faine would arive, but cannot for the storme,
  If too great winde against the port him drive,
  Doth in the port it selfe his vessell rive.

XXII

When that brave honour of the Latine name,
Which mear'd her rule with Africa and Byze,
With Thames inhabitants of noble fame,
And they which see the dawning day arize,
Her nourslings did with mutinous uprore
Harten against her selfe, her conquer'd spoile,
Which she had wonne from all the world afore,
Of all the world was spoyl'd within a while:
So, when the compast course of the universe
In sixe and thirtie thousand yeares is ronne,
The bands of th'elements shall backe reverse
To their first discord, and be quite undonne;
  The seedes of which all things at first were bred
  Shall in great Chaos wombe againe be hid.

XXIII

O warie wisedome of the man that would
That Carthage towres from spoile should be forborne,
To th'end that his victorious people should
With cancring laisure not be overworne!
He well foresaw how that the Romane courage,
Impatient of pleasures faint desires,
Through idlenes would turne to civill rage,
And be her selfe the matter of her fires.
For in a people given all to ease,
Ambition is engendred easily;
As, in a vicious bodie, grose disease
Soone growes through humours superfluitie.
  That came to passe, when, swolne with plenties pride,
  Nor prince, nor peere, nor kin, they would abide.

XXIV

If the blinde Furie which warres breedeth oft
Wonts not t'enrage the hearts of equall beasts,
Whether they fare on foote, or flie aloft,
Or armed be with clawes, or scalie creasts,
What fell Erynnis, with hot burning tongs,
Did grype your hearts with noysome rage imbew'd,
That, each to other working cruell wrongs,
Your blades in your owne bowels you embrew'd ?
Was this, ye Romanes, your hard destinie?
Or some old sinne, whose unappeased guilt
Powr'd vengeance forth on you eternallie?
Or brothers blood, the which at first was spilt
  Upon your walls, that God might not endure
  Upon the same to set foundation sure?

XXV

O that I had the Thracian poets harpe,
For to awake out of th'infernall shade
Those antique Caesars, sleeping long in darke,
The which this auncient citie whilome made!
Or that I had Amphions instrument,
To quicken with his vitall notes accord
The stonie ioynts of these old walls now rent,
By which th'Ausonian light might be restor'd !
Or that at least I could with pencill fine
Fashion the pourtraicts of these palacis,
By paterne of great Virgils spirit divine!
I would assay with that which in me is
  To builde, with levell of my loftie style,
  That which no hands can evermore compyle.

XXVI

Who list the Romane greatnes forth to figure,
Him needeth not to seeke for usage right
Of line, or lead, or rule, or squaire, to measure
Her length, her breadth, her deepnes, or her hight;
But him behooves to vew in compasse round
All that the ocean graspes in his long armes;
Be it where the yerely starre doth scortch the ground,
Or where colde Boreas blowes his bitter stormes.
Rome was th'whole world, and al the world was Rome;
And if things nam'd their names doo equalize,
When land and sea ye name, then name ye Rome,
And, naming Rome, ye land and sea comprize:
  For th'auncient plot of Rome, displayed plaine,
  The map of all the wide world doth containe.

XXVII

Thou that at Rome astonisht dost behold
The antique pride which menaced the skie,
These haughtie heapes, these palaces of olde,
These wals, these arcks, these baths, these temples his,
Iudge, by these ample ruines vew, the rest
The which iniurious time hath quite outworne,
Since, of all workmen helde in reckning best,
Yet these olde fragments are for paternes borne:
Then also marke how Rome, from day to day,
Repayring her decayed fashion,
Renewes herselfe with buildings rich and gay;
That one would iudge that the Romaine Daemon
  Doth yet himselfe with fatall hand enforce
  Againe on foot to reare her pouldred corse.

XXVIII

He that hath seene a great oke drie and dead,
Yet clad with reliques of some trophees olde,
Lifting to heaven her aged hoarie head,
Whose foote in ground hath left but feeble holde,
But halfe disbowel'd lies above the ground,
Shewing her wreathed rootes, and naked armes,
And on her trunke all rotten and unsound
Onely supports herselfe for meate of wormes,
And, though she owe her fall to the first winde,
Yet of the devout people is ador'd,
And manie yong plants spring out of her rinde;
Who such an oke hath seene, let him record
  That such this cities honour was of yore,
  And mongst all cities florished much more.

XXIX

All that which Aegypt whilome did devise,
All that which Greece their temples to embrave,
After th'Ionicke, Atticke, Doricke guise,
Or Corinth skil'd in curious workes to grave,
All that Lysippus practike arte could forme,
Apelles wit, or Phidias his skill,
Was wont this auncient citie to adorne,
And the heaven it selfe with her wide wonders fill.
All that which Athens ever brought forth wise,
All that which Afrike ever brought forth strange,
All that which Asie ever had of prise,
Was here to see. O mervelous great change!
  Rome, living, was the worlds sole ornament;
  And, dead, is now the worlds sole moniment.

XXX

Like as the seeded field greene grasse first showes,
Then from greene grasse into a stalke doth spring,
And from a stalke into an eare forth-growes,
Which eare the frutefull graine doth shortly bring,
And as in season due the husband mowes
The waving lockes of those faire yeallow heares,
Which, bound in sheaves, and layd in comely rowes,
Upon the naked fields in stalkes he reares,
So grew the Romane empire by degree,
Till that barbarian hands it quite did spill,
And left of it but these olde markes to see,
Of which all passers by doo somewhat pill,
  As they which gleane, the reliques use to gather
  Which th'husbandman behind him chanst to scater.

XXXI

That same is now nought but a champian wide,
Where all this worlds pride once was situate.
No blame to thee, whosoever dost abide
By Nyle, or Gange, or Tygre, or Euphrate;
Ne Afrike thereof guiltie is, nor Spaine,
Nor the bolde people by the Thamis brincks,
Nor the brave warlicke brood of Alemaine,
Nor the borne souldier which Rhine running drinks.
Thou onely cause, O Civill Furie, art!
Which, sowing in th'Aemathian fields thy spight,
Didst arme thy hand against thy proper hart;
To th'end that when thou wast in greatest hight
  To greatnes growne, through long prosperitie,
  Thou then adowne might'st fall more horriblie.

XXXII

Hope ye, my Verses, that posteritie
Of age ensuing shall you ever read?
Hope ye that ever immortalitie
So meane harpes worke may chalenge for her meed?
If under heaven anie endurance were,
These moniments, which not in paper writ,
But in porphyre and marble doo appeare,
Might well have hop'd to have obtained it.
Nath'les, my Lute, whom Phoebus deigned to give,
Cease not to sound these olde antiquities:
For if that Time doo let thy glorie live,
Well maist thou boast, how ever base thou bee,
  That thou art first which of thy nation song
  Th'olde honour of the people gowned long.

L'ENVOY

Bellay, first garland of free poesie
That France brought forth, though fruitfull of brave wits,
Well worthie thou of immortalitie,
That long hast traveld, by thy learned writs,
Olde Rome out of her ashes to revive,
And give a second life to dead decayes!
Needes must he all eternitie survive,
That can to other give eternall dayes.
Thy dayes therefore are endles, and thy prayse
Excelling all that ever went before:
And, after thee, gins Bartas hie to rayse
His heavenly Muse, th'Almightie to adore.
  Live happie spirits, th'honour of your name,
  And fill the world with never dying fame!

William Etty, Britomart Redeems Faire Amoret, 1833, Tate Gallery

Briton Rivière, Una and the Lion, from The Fairie Queene

John Henry Fuseli, from The Faire Queene, 1788, Basel

John Hamilton Mortimer, Sir Arthegal, the Knight of Justice,
Faerie Queene, Tate Gallery

Florimell Saved By Proteus, by Walter Crane, 1895-97

Edmund Spenser's Faerie Queene, an edition from 1895

A Note On Edmund Spenser

by Teresa Page

Edmund Spenser created a drama of England in his poetry. The 'dream' occurs throughout his poetry, but finds its most concentrated expression in *The Faerie Queene*, with its epic treatment of the 'dream of Albion', a myth-making vision of Blighty as the expression of Elizabeth I's magnificence, and vice versa. *The Faerie Queene* is an astonishing work, by any standards, and it dwarfs, at times, even those other creations of the Renaissance that are so revered by readers and critics – Marlowe's *Doctor Faustus*, Shakespeare's plays and Sidney's *Astrophel and Stella*.

Elizabeth I appropriated the cult of the Virgin Mary, styling herself as the Virgin Queen of an Empire, according to Frances Yates:

> *The bejewelled and painted images of the Virgin Mary had been cast out of churches and monasteries, but another bejewelled and painted image was set up in court, and went in progress through the land for her worshippers to adore. The cult of the Virgin was regarded as one of the chief abuses of the unreformed Church, but it would be, perhaps, extravagant to suggest that, in a Christian country, the worship of the state Virgo was deliberately intended to take its place.*[1]

This changeover from Catholic to Anglican allegiance is nothing new: many other monarchs and leaders have appropriated some mass feeling or politics for their own purposes. The power and influence of Elizabeth I and her 'nearly fifty years of myth-making', as Steve Davies puts it,[2] extended through the ages. It did not stop with her death; as Maureen Sabine explains how Elizabeth and her court rewrote Christianity, so the Queen of Heaven became the Queen of Britain:

> *Immediately upon her coronation, she took steps to suppress the belief that the mass was an offering of the true body of Christ which had really issued from the body of the Virgin Mary. In subsuming not only Corpus Christi but the fears of Mary to the propaganda of her provident rule, she made it clear that it was no longer Christ and his Mother but her body which constituted the immutable and vernal life of the church. her tenacious hold over English social life as reigning queen for nearly fifty years, her remarkable longevity and robustness of person and her immersion in the Marian role of ageless virgin-mother-spouse consecrated to her people helped to substantiate this monumental lie.*[3]

There are many areas that are fascinating but too involved to deal with here: Edmund Spenser's relation to Queen Elizabeth, his use of the mythology of Elizabeth, the relation between his use of Classic mythology and contemporary British royal mythology, his use of pastoral imagery, the sociological and political picture presented in *The Faerie Queene*, the relation between Spenser and Shakespeare, between Spenser and courtly love poetry, between Spenser and Christianity, etc.[4]

The poem 'April', from *The Shepheardes Calendar*, in this book, is an extraordinary hymn to Elizabeth I, full of many poetic pleasures. It is an ecologue, as Simon Shepherd notes, that barely hides its sexism and patriarchal power relations:

> *The reader – who is assumed, crucially, to be male – is given a position of power which is constructed from the idea of viewing. A woman is decorated by a male text and looked at by a male readership as an object. The male poet's skill brings into being this decorated woman. The (male) reader consents to imagine and respond to the poet's vision.* (32)

This occurs in most poetry: in Petrarch's *Canzoniere*, or

Shakespeare's *Sonnets*, or Sidney's *Astrophel and Stella*, Keats' *Odes* or Goethe's lyrics the reader is assumed to be male. It happens in painting, where the subject is 'feminine' (the female nude, or the pastoral landscape, which is a Goddess, the Mother Earth). The subject is an object of pleasure, promising Arcadian delights. The viewer of 'high art' paintings is presumed to be male. It is a case of the male gaze controlling the female object of desire. Simon Shepherd continues:

> *Although pleasurable, this reader's position is clearly false. The hymn does not exhibit the language of Elizabethan myth, it employs its power… In brief, the hymn has been written by a poet whose 'mynd was alienate', and it is sung by his former but now rejected friend. While the text of the hymn celebrates fullness, its creator and performer are both frustrated and distressed. The glorification of Elisa/ Elizabeth need not presuppose the content of the glorifiers.* (32-3)

In *The Faerie Queene* section included here, the frame is a mythical quest or journey. The pleasure is in following the hero on his quest, as in Arthurian legend. This is, again, a particularly masculine pleasure, as found in the masculinist pursuits of chivalry, hunting, courtly love, etc.

Technically, Edmund Spenser knew everything about poetry, it seems. He wrote many sonnets, and in his *The Faerie Queene* he wrote hundreds of nine-line stanzas. There is a stately progress to Spenser's poesie: he did not rush things. He took his time. Wordsworth spoke of

> *Sweet Spenser, moving through his clouded heaven*
> *With the moon's beauty and the moon's soft pace*

In the *Amoretti*, Edmund Spenser tackled his target, his beloved, from many directions, as Michael Spiller notes in his excellent survey of the sonnet form:

> *Spenser, then, creates in the Amoretti an /I/ who desires one thing*

(marriage to his Lady) but performs his desire eloquently from various angels and in various voices and registers, within the range conventional to the sonnet discourse. So there is affectionate badinage (lxxi), erotic fantasia (lxxvi), anecdote (lxxv), self-reproach (lxxxiv), ironic conversation with others (xxix), extravagant addresses to Cupid (x) and moral commonplaces (xxvi); there are sonnets which address the Lady, others which talk about her, others which are private self-communings, even ones which have Sidney's (and Wyatt's) trick of suggesting a conversation in progress (xxxiii, lxv). There is also a variety of emotions directed towards the beloved: exasperation (x), adoration (viii), frustration (xxxvi), rage (lxvi), sexual desire (lxiv), companionship (lxxv), avuncular consolation (lxvi), loneliness (lxxxvii) and joy (lxxxii).[5]

Edmund Spenser is unsurpassed in the art of poetic exaltation – no other poet of the era – and of subsequent or previous eras – attains Spenser's sense of the superlative, the exalted. Spenser's poetry is a litany of pæans: 'Epithalamion', 'A Hymn in Honour of Love', 'A Hymn in Honour of Beauty', 'A Hymn of Heavenly Beauty', 'A Hymn of Heavenly Love', 'Prothalamion', 'The Shepheardes Calendar' and of course *The Faerie Queene* all contain passages of lyrical praise. Like Shakespeare, Spenser's view of the world as crystallized in his poetry is an expansive, dramatic, encyclopædic vision. The sheer amount of work by Spenser – the copious letters, 'Complaints', 'Hymns', sonnets, and stanzas in *The Faerie Queene* attest to his love of writing. The length of *The Faerie Queene* is not the least astonishing thing about it. Spenser clearly had a lot to say, and would not stop until he had said it. Works such as 'The Shepheardes Calendar' are also very long, while shorter pieces (for Spenser), such as the 'Epithalamion', are, by today's standards, lengthy works. This makes the entirety of Spenser's *œuvre* difficult to grasp, so all-encompassing is it, yet this is also partly why he is so central to English literature. Few other poets have written at such length and in such detail (one thinks of Shakespeare with his 37 or so plays, Dante and his *Divina Commedia*, and the long poem sequences of Milton, Shelley, Marlowe and Wordsworth). Length does not equal quality, but Spenser's range is so large, his learning so encyclopædic (he recalls Sir Thomas Browne or John Dee in this respect) and his sense of occasion and detail so acute, his work remains, with Shakespeare, Chaucer, Wordsworth and Milton, absolutely the apotheosis of English poetry.

NOTES

1. Frances Yates, *Giordano Bruno and the Hermetic Tradition*, London 1964. See also Frances Yates: *The Rosicrucian Enlightenment*, Routledge 1972; Ted Hughes: *Shakespeare and the Goddess of Complete Being*, Faber 1992;D.P. Walker: *Spiritual and Demonic Magic from Ficino to Campanella*, Warburg Institute 1958; Wayne Shumaker: *The Occult Sciences in the Renaissance*, University of California Press, Berkeley, Calif., 1972; Walter Pagel: *Paracelsus: An Introduction to Philosophical Medicine in the Era of the Renaissance*, Karger, New York 1958; Peter French: *John Dee*, Routledge 1972

2. Stevie Davies: *The Idea of Woman in Renaissance Literature: The Feminine Reclaimed*, Harvester Press, Brighton 1986

3. Maureen Sabine: *Feminine Engendered Faith: The Poetry of John Donne and Richard Crashaw*, Macmillan 1992, 13

4. See, for starters: Louise Montrose: ""Eliza, Queene of Shepheardes" and the Pastoral of Power", in *English Language Review*, vol. X, 1980, 164-6; Elkin Calhoun Wilson: *England's Eliza*, Harvard Studies in English, vol. XX, Octagon, New York 1966; Robin Wells: *Spenser's Faerie Queene and the Cult of Elizabeth*, Barnes & Noble, Totowa, New Jersey 1983; Adrian Morey: *The Catholic Subjects of Elizabeth I*, Allen & Unwin 1978; William P. Haugaard: *Elizabeth and the English Reformation: The Struggle for a Stable Settlement of Religion*, Cambridge University Press, 1968; Margaret Ferguson *et al*, eds: *Rewriting the Renaissance: The Discourses of Sexual Difference in Early Modern Europe*, University of Chicago Press 1986; Carole Levin: "Power, politics, and sexuality: images of Elizabeth I", in Jean R. Brink *et al*, eds: *The Politics of Gender in Early Modern, Sixteenth Century Studies and Essays*, 12, 1989, 95-110; Leonard Tennenhouse: *Power on Display: The Politics of Shakespeare's Genres*, Methuen 1986; Roy Strong: *The Cult of Elizabeth I*, Thames & Hudson 1977

5. Michael R.G. Spiller: *The Development of the Sonnet: An Introduction*, Routledge 1992, 148

FURTHER READING

I have provided some further reading for Spenser's work, and for the art of the Elizabethan sonnet below.

For books on the sonnet, those by Michael Spiller and Sandra Berman are excellent. Heather Dubrow's study of the sonnet form and the influence of Francesco Petrarch on English poetry is superb. J.W. Lever's and Maurice Valency's books are classics.

Sandra Berman. *The Sonnet Over Time*, Chapel Hill, 1988
Jean R. Brink *et al*, eds: *The Politics of Gender in Early Modern, Sixteenth Century Studies and Essays*, 12, 1989
Reed Way Dasenbrock. *Imitating the Italians: Wyatt, Spenser, Syne, Pound, Joyce*, John Hopkins University Press, Baltimore, 1991
Stevie Davies: *The Idea of Woman in Renaissance Literature: The Feminine Reclaimed*, Harvester Press, Brighton 1986
Heather Dubrow. *Echoes of Desire: English Petrarchism and Its Counterdiscourses*, Cornell University Press, 1995
Maurice Evans, ed. *Elizabethan Sonnets*, Dent, 1977
Margaret Ferguson. *Trials of Desire: Renaissance Defenses of Poetry*, Yale University Press, New Haven, 1983
—. *et al*, eds. *Rewriting the Renaissance*, University of Chicago Press, 1986
Anne Ferry. *The "Inward" Language: Sonnets of Wyatt, Sidney, Shakespeare, Donne*, University of Chicago Press, 1983
William P. Haugaard: *Elizabeth and the English Reformation: The Struggle for a Stable Settlement of Religion*, Cambridge University Press, 1968
Jane Hedley. *Power in Verse: Metaphor and Metonymy in the Renaissance*

Lyric, Pennsylvania State University Press University Park, 1988

J.W. Lever. *The Elizabethan Love Sonnet*, Methuen, 1956

Arthur Marotti. ""Love is not love": Elizabethan Sonnet Sequences and the Social Order", *English Literary History*, 49, 1982

Louise Montrose: ""Eliza, Queene of Shepheardes" and the Pastoral of Power", in *English Language Review*, vol. X, 1980, 164-6

Adrian Morey: *The Catholic Subjects of Elizabeth I*, Allen & Unwin 1978

Maureen Sabine: *Feminine Engendered Faith: The Poetry of John Donne and Richard Crashaw*, Macmillan 1992

Michael R.G. Spiller: *The Development of the Sonnet: An introduction*, Routledge 1992

Roy Strong: *The Cult of Elizabeth I*, Thames & Hudson 1977

Leonard Tennenhouse: *Power on Display: The Politics of Shakespeare's Genres*, Methuen 1986

Maurice Valency. *In Praise of Love: An Introduction to the Love-Poetry of the Renaissance*, Macmillan, New York, 1961

Robin Wells: *Spenser's Faerie Queene and the Cult of Elizabeth*, Barnes & Noble, Totowa, New Jersey 1983

Elkin Calhoun Wilson: *England's Eliza*, Harvard Studies in English, vol. XX, Octagon, New York 1966

In the Dim Void

Samuel Beckett's Late Trilogy: *Company, Ill Seen, Ill Said* and *Worstward Ho*

by Gregory Johns

This book discusses the luminous beauty and dense, rigorous poetry of Samuel Beckett's late works, *Company, Ill Seen, Ill Said* and *Worstward Ho*. Gregory Johns looks back over Beckett's long writing career, charting the development from the *Molloy-Malone Dies-Unnamable* trilogy through the 'fizzles' of the 1960s to the elegiac lyricism of the *Company* series. Johns compares the trilogy with late plays such as *Ghosts, Footfalls* and *Rockaby*.

Bibliography, notes. Illustrated. 120pp
ISBN 9781861712974 Pbk and ISBN 9781861712608 Hbk
9781861713407 E-book

Life, Life
Selected Poems

Arseny Tarkovsky

translated and edited by Virginia Rounding

Arseny Tarkovsky is the neglected Russian poet, father of the acclaimed film director Andrei Tarkovsky. This new book gathers together many of Tarkovsky's most lyrical and heartfelt poems, in Rounding's clear, new translations. Many of Tarkovsky's poems appeared in his son's films, such as *Mirror, Stalker, Nostalghia* and *The Sacrifice*.
There is an introduction by Rounding, and a bibliography of both Arseny and Andrei Tarkovsky.

Bibliography and notes 124pp 3rd ed   ISBN 9781861712660 Hbk   ISBN 9781861711144

MAURICE SENDAK
& the art of children's book illustration

Maurice Sendak is the widely acclaimed American children's book author and illustrator. This critical study focuses on his famous trilogy, *Where the Wild Things Are, In the Night Kitchen* and *Outside Over There*, as well as the early works and Sendak's superb depictions of the Grimm Brothers' fairy tales in *The Juniper Tree*. L.M. Poole begins with a chapter on children's book illustration, in particular the treatment of fairy tales. Sendak's work is situated within the history of children's book illustration, and he is compared with many contemporary authors.

Fully illustrated. The book has been revised and updated for this edition.
ISBN 9781861714282 Pbk   ISBN 9781861713469 Hbk

Beauties, Beasts, and Enchantment

CLASSIC FRENCH FAIRY TALES

Translated and with an Introduction by Jack Zipes

A collection of 36 classic French fairy tales translated by renowned writer Jack Zipes. *Cinderella*, *Beauty and the Beast*, *Sleeping Beauty* and *Little Red Riding Hood* are among the classic fairy tales in this amazing book.
Includes illustrations from fairy tale collections.
Jack Zipes has written and published widely on fairy tales.

'Terrific... a succulent array of 17th and 18th century 'salon' fairy tales'
- *The New York Times Book Review*

'These tales are adventurous, thrilling in a way fairy tales are meant to be... The translation from the French is modern, happily free of archaic and hyperbolic language... a fine and sophisticated collection' - *New York Tribune*

'Enjoyable to read... a unique collection of French regional folklore' - *Library Journal*

'Charming stories accompanied by attractive pen-and-ink drawings' - *Chattanooga Times*

Introduction and illustrations   612pp.   ISBN 9781861712510 Pbk   ISBN 9781861713193 Hbk

CRESCENT MOON PUBLISHING

web: www.crmoon.com e-mail: cresmopub@yahoo.co.uk

ARTS, PAINTING, SCULPTURE

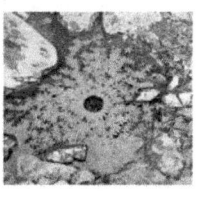

The Art of Andy Goldsworthy
Andy Goldsworthy: Touching Nature
Andy Goldsworthy in Close-Up
Andy Goldsworthy: Pocket Guide
Andy Goldsworthy In America
Land Art: A Complete Guide
The Art of Richard Long
Richard Long: Pocket Guide
Land Art In the UK
Land Art in Close-Up
Land Art In the U.S.A.
Land Art: Pocket Guide
Installation Art in Close-Up
Minimal Art and Artists In the 1960s and After
Colourfield Painting
Land Art DVD, TV documentary
Andy Goldsworthy DVD, TV documentary
The Erotic Object: Sexuality in Sculpture From Prehistory to the Present Day
Sex in Art: Pornography and Pleasure in Painting and Sculpture
Postwar Art
Sacred Gardens: The Garden in Myth, Religion and Art
Glorification: Religious Abstraction in Renaissance and 20th Century Art
Early Netherlandish Painting
Leonardo da Vinci
Piero della Francesca
Giovanni Bellini

Fra Angelico: Art and Religion in the Renaissance
Mark Rothko: The Art of Transcendence
Frank Stella: American Abstract Artist
Jasper Johns
Brice Marden

Alison Wilding: The Embrace of Sculpture
Vincent van Gogh: Visionary Landscapes
Eric Gill: Nuptials of God
Constantin Brancusi: Sculpting the Essence of Things
Max Beckmann
Caravaggio
Gustave Moreau
Egon Schiele: Sex and Death In Purple Stockings
Delizioso Fotografico Fervore: Works In Process 1
Sacro Cuore: Works In Process 2
The Light Eternal: J.M.W. Turner
The Madonna Glorified: Karen Arthurs

LITERATURE

J.R.R. Tolkien: The Books, The Films, The Whole Cultural Phenomenon
J.R.R. Tolkien: Pocket Guide
Tolkien's Heroic Quest
The *Earthsea* Books of Ursula Le Guin
Beauties, Beasts and Enchantment: Classic French Fairy Tales
German Popular Stories by the Brothers Grimm
Philip Pullman and *His Dark Materials*
Sexing Hardy: Thomas Hardy and Feminism
Thomas Hardy's *Tess of the d'Urbervilles*
Thomas Hardy's *Jude the Obscure*
Thomas Hardy: The Tragic Novels
Love and Tragedy: Thomas Hardy
The Poetry of Landscape in Hardy
Wessex Revisited: Thomas Hardy and John Cowper Powys
Wolfgang Iser: Essays and Interviews
Petrarch, Dante and the Troubadours
Maurice Sendak and the Art of Children's Book Illustration
Andrea Dworkin
Cixous, Irigaray, Kristeva: The *Jouissance* of French Feminism
Julia Kristeva: Art, Love, Melancholy, Philosophy, Semiotics and Psychoanalysis
Hélene Cixous I Love You: The *Jouissance* of Writing
Luce Irigaray: Lips, Kissing, and the Politics of Sexual Difference
Peter Redgrove: Here Comes the Flood
Peter Redgrove: Sex-Magic-Poetry-Cornwall
Lawrence Durrell: Between Love and Death, East and West
Love, Culture & Poetry: Lawrence Durrell
Cavafy: Anatomy of a Soul
German Romantic Poetry: Goethe, Novalis, Heine, Hölderlin
Feminism and Shakespeare
Shakespeare: Love, Poetry & Magic
The Passion of D.H. Lawrence
D.H. Lawrence: Symbolic Landscapes
D.H. Lawrence: Infinite Sensual Violence
Rimbaud: Arthur Rimbaud and the Magic of Poetry
The Ecstasies of John Cowper Powys
Sensualism and Mythology: The Wessex Novels of John Cowper Powys
Amorous Life: John Cowper Powys and the Manifestation of Affectivity (H.W. Fawkner)
Postmodern Powys: New Essays on John Cowper Powys (Joe Boulter)
Rethinking Powys: Critical Essays on John Cowper Powys
Paul Bowles & Bernardo Bertolucci
Rainer Maria Rilke
Joseph Conrad: *Heart of Darkness*
In the Dim Void: Samuel Beckett
Samuel Beckett Goes into the Silence
André Gide: Fiction and Fervour
Jackie Collins and the Blockbuster Novel
Blinded By Her Light: The Love-Poetry of Robert Graves
The Passion of Colours: Travels In Mediterranean Lands
Poetic Forms

POETRY

Ursula Le Guin: Walking In Cornwall
Peter Redgrove: Here Comes The Flood
Peter Redgrove: Sex-Magic-Poetry-Cornwall
Dante: Selections From the Vita Nuova
Petrarch, Dante and the Troubadours
William Shakespeare: Sonnets
William Shakespeare: Complete Poems
Blinded By Her Light: The Love-Poetry of Robert Graves
Emily Dickinson: Selected Poems
Emily Brontë: Poems
Thomas Hardy: Selected Poems
Percy Bysshe Shelley: Poems
John Keats: Selected Poems
Joh n Keats: Poems of 1820
D.H. Lawrence: Selected Poems
Edmund Spenser: Poems
Edmund Spenser: Amoretti
John Donne: Poems
Henry Vaughan: Poems
Sir Thomas Wyatt: Poems
Robert Herrick: Selected Poems
Rilke: Space, Essence and Angels in the Poetry of Rainer Maria Rilke
Rainer Maria Rilke: Selected Poems
Friedrich Hölderlin: Selected Poems
Arseny Tarkovsky: Selected Poems
Arthur Rimbaud: Selected Poems
Arthur Rimbaud: A Season in Hell
Arthur Rimbaud and the Magic of Poetry
Novalis: Hymns To the Night
German Romantic Poetry
Paul Verlaine: Selected Poems
Elizaethan Sonnet Cycles
D.J. Enright: By-Blows
Jeremy Reed: Brigitte's Blue Heart
Jeremy Reed: Claudia Schiffer's Red Shoes
Gorgeous Little Orpheus
Radiance: New Poems
Crescent Moon Book of Nature Poetry
Crescent Moon Book of Love Poetry
Crescent Moon Book of Mystical Poetry
Crescent Moon Book of Elizabethan Love Poetry
Crescent Moon Book of Metaphysical Poetry
Crescent Moon Book of Romantic Poetry
Pagan America: New American Poetry

MEDIA, CINEMA, FEMINISM and CULTURAL STUDIES

J.R.R. Tolkien: The Books, The Films, The Whole Cultural Phenomenon
J.R.R. Tolkien: Pocket Guide
The *Lord of the Rings* Movies: Pocket Guide
The Cinema of Hayao Miyazaki
Hayao Miyazaki: *Princess Mononoke*: Pocket Movie Guide
Hayao Miyazaki: *Spirited Away*: Pocket Movie Guide
Tim Burton : Hallowe'en For Hollywood
Ken Russell
Ken Russell: *Tommy*: Pocket Movie Guide
The Ghost Dance: The Origins of Religion
The Peyote Cult
Cixous, Irigaray, Kristeva: The *Jouissance* of French Feminism
Julia Kristeva: Art, Love, Melancholy, Philosophy, Semiotics and Psychoanalysis
Luce Irigaray: Lips, Kissing, and the Politics of Sexual Difference
Hélene Cixous I Love You: The *Jouissance* of Writing
Andrea Dworkin
'Cosmo Woman': The World of Women's Magazines
Women in Pop Music
HomeGround: The Kate Bush Anthology
Discovering the Goddess (Geoffrey Ashe)
The Poetry of Cinema
The Sacred Cinema of Andrei Tarkovsky
Andrei Tarkovsky: Pocket Guide
Andrei Tarkovsky: *Mirror*: Pocket Movie Guide
Andrei Tarkovsky: *The Sacrifice*: Pocket Movie Guide
Walerian Borowczyk: Cinema of Erotic Dreams
Jean-Luc Godard: The Passion of Cinema
Jean-Luc Godard: *Hail Mary*: Pocket Movie Guide
Jean-Luc Godard: *Contempt*: Pocket Movie Guide
Jean-Luc Godard: *Pierrot le Fou*: Pocket Movie Guide
John Hughes and Eighties Cinema
Ferris Bueller's Day Off: Pocket Movie Guide
Jean-Luc Godard: Pocket Guide
The Cinema of Richard Linklater
Liv Tyler: Star In Ascendance
Blade Runner and the Films of Philip K. Dick
Paul Bowles and Bernardo Bertolucci
Media Hell: Radio, TV and the Press
An Open Letter to the BBC
Detonation Britain: Nuclear War in the UK
Feminism and Shakespeare
Wild Zones: Pornography, Art and Feminism
Sex in Art: Pornography and Pleasure in Painting and Sculpture
Sexing Hardy: Thomas Hardy and Feminism

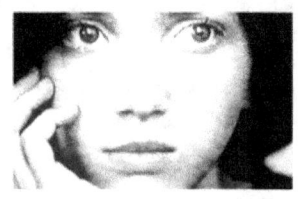

The Light Eternal is a model monograph, an exemplary job. The subject matter of the book is beautifully organised and dead on beam. (Lawrence Durrell)

It is amazing for me to see my work treated with such passion and respect. (Andrea Dworkin)

CRESCENT MOON PUBLISHING
P.O. Box 1312, Maidstone, Kent, ME14 5XU, Great Britain. www.crmoon.com

cresmopub@yahoo.co.uk   www.crescentmoon.org.uk

www.ingramcontent.com/pod-product-compliance
Lightning Source LLC
Chambersburg PA
CBHW071403080526
44587CB00017B/3167